| PILGRIM · GUIDE |

YORK

Also available in the *Pilgrim Guide* series

PILGRIM · GUIDE

YORK

Leslie Stanbridge

and

John Toy

CANTERBURY
PRESS
Norwich

Text © Leslie Stanbridge and John Toy 1997
Illustrations © Jeremy Muldowney 1997

First published in 1997 by The Canterbury Press Norwich
(a publishing imprint of Hymns Ancient & Modern Limited,
a registered charity)
St Mary's Works, St Mary's Plain,
Norwich, Norfolk NR3 3BH

Leslie Stanbridge and John Toy have asserted their right under the
Copyright, Designs and Patents Act 1988, to be identified as Authors of
this Work

British Library Cataloguing in Publication Data

A catalogue record for this book is available
from the British Library

ISBN 1-85311-167-8

*Typeset and printed in Great Britain by The Lavenham Press Ltd,
Lavenham, Suffolk, CO10 9RN*

Contents

Acknowledgements

The plan of York Minster on page 30 is by Timo Little.

Prayers by Angela Ashwin are reproduced from *The Book of a Thousand Prayers*, by permission of HarperCollins Publishers Ltd.

Page 43   The Mothers' Union prayer is published by permission of the Mothers' Union.

Page 45   Prayer reproduced by permission of the Conference of European Churches.

Page 55   Prayer by George Appleton reproduced by permission of Cassell Publishers Ltd. Prayer by Mother Teresa is taken from *Something Beautiful For God*, Malcolm Muggeridge and reproduced by permission of Harper Collins Publishers Ltd.

A Pilgrimage Prayer

Thank you, Father, for this ancient place of prayer;
    for the faith that has blossomed here,
    and for the worship in all seasons offered here;
    for the lives that have been touched here,
    and commitment stirred into life here.
As we tread in the footsteps of our mothers and fathers in
    the faith,
    bless us and all who come here,
    and speak to us with the whisper of your love;
    for you are a God of renewal and of steadfastness,
    now and for ever.

© Angela Ashwin 1996

Cathedral

Let us construct the finest House, they said.
No expense spared. It will take generations.
Specialists came from all around. Great men arose
who gave voice to the new project,
showed the way. It must inspire, inform
and enchant, they said, or it is nothing.
It should in every way point to him
who is over all and in all. The whole
should be a tapestry of dazzling contrasts
and incomparable details, evoking wonder
and praise. Pilgrimages should have
an earthbound destination as matchless
as the celestial Cause. No other house
could have such a story to tell:
here there was knowledge of salvation.
And again was heard the ageless echo: 'Thy will be done'.

© John Angus 1993

Authors' Preface

The main part of this book (pages 30–57) is the pilgrim route round the floor of the Minster (open; no charge; donation invited), following mainly the route taken by most visitors. It is designed so that you can use it on your own or in a small group. It enables a visit to the Minster to be a Christian act of prayer and not just a visit to see architecture, monuments or stained glass. Numerals in square brackets, such as [5], refer to those in the Plan of the Minster – see page 30.

Since such a route has to dodge about historically, however, the first part of the book (pages 12–29) is a brief chronological history of the site from Roman times until today. The site was important before the present Gothic cathedral was built, and extensive remains of the earlier buildings can be seen in the Foundations and crypts (entrance charge). The four sections dealing with the prehistory of the site are provided with suggestions of prayers so that visits can also be made prayerfully.

The book concludes with a circular pilgrim tour round some of the churches and other sites in York north of the river.

What is pilgrimage?

To be a Christian is to follow 'the way' of Christ. All through the Bible people are on the move – Abraham, the Israelites in the wilderness, and the exiles going to Babylon; and then Jesus himself, never settling down, and finally coming to God's city, Jerusalem, there to be crucified and raised from the dead.

The Christian therefore is a pilgrim and needs outward and visible things to help him or her on this pilgrimage; the sacraments are the obvious examples, but they can be supplemented by many different aids. Going to places where Christ lived is one of them, and all down the ages pilgrims have gone to the holy places in Palestine, especially Bethlehem, Galilee and Jerusalem. But not all could go that far, and in the Middle Ages many journeyed to places made holy by the relics of saints and the memories of their lives. In this country, Becket's shrine at Canterbury was a favourite, and in the north-east, Lindisfarne, Durham, Beverley, Howden and York. Pilgrims went to pray, often seeking healing for themselves or for others.

Gradually superstition became attached to pilgrim shrines, and in the later Middle Ages there was much criticism of pilgrimages; in countries where the Reformation prospered shrines were dismantled and pilgrimages stopped, and the idea was spiritualized (as in Bunyan's *Pilgrim's Progress*).

Today the practice has been re-born. Many have discovered the joy of pilgrimage by visits to the Holy Land, and then have begun to seek out pilgrim places nearer at hand, places made holy by generations of saintly Christians. Among them is York Minster.

If pilgrimage reflects the daily journeyings of Jesus, it can also reflect our own daily journeys, for all our lives can be seen as pilgrimages. So if we visit a holy place, it is in order to make every place and every time holy. Pilgrimage also reflects on the end of life. According to Bede's *History of the Church*, this is what one of King Edwin's counsellors said to him when in 627 he was considering becoming a Christian:

> *Your Majesty, when we compare the present life of man with that of the time of which we have no knowledge, it seems to me like the swift flight of a lone sparrow through the banqueting hall … Inside there is a comforting fire to warm the room; outside the wintry storms of snow and rain are raging. The sparrow flies swiftly in through one door of the hall, and out through another… Similarly man appears on earth for a little while, but we know nothing of what went before this life and what follows. Therefore if this new teaching can reveal any more certain knowledge, it seems only right that we should follow it.*

He decided to follow this way and was baptized in York in the first Minster built for the purpose. In the place where he, and countless others, have taken this step, let us enrich our own life's pilgrimage in quiet enjoyment and silent prayer.

The first four sections of this introduction concern the site before the present cathedral was built and therefore do not correspond with anything that can be seen on the floor of the Minster where the main pilgrimage (pp 30–57) takes place. Accordingly, locations and prayers are suggested for these so that each may be treated prayerfully when visited. For the remaining sections no locations are given since they are covered in the main pilgrimage, but a prayer appropriate to the century concerned is included.

The beginning of York and its Christians

1st–5th centuries

Suggested location: *In the Foundations among the Roman ruins, especially in the south or west chambers.*

When the Romans arrived here in AD72 the ground north of the river became the fortress for the army garrison. Here were the army barrack blocks, and in the middle (where the central tower of the Minster now stands) was the assembly hall for the legionaries. Here in July 306 Constantine was acclaimed as Emperor by his troops on the death in York of his father, the Emperor Constantius. Six years later Constantine (called the Great) declared Christianity to be a permitted religion, ending the two centuries of persecution. Churches could be built for the first time and faith openly expressed. Christian Europe had begun!

There were Christians in York in those times; we know this because one of their bishops, named Eborius in the records, travelled to southern France for the first General Council of the Church at Arles in AD314. The Christian faith would have been brought here by traders and perhaps missionaries, and

12

the Church must have grown in strength after Constantine. It probably outlasted the departure of the Romans from York around AD410 but not for much longer.

Thank God for the endurance of all persecuted Christians in every age and for those who have defended them and allowed the Christian Church to flourish. Thank him also for the faith of those pioneer Christians in this place in those far-off days and for the influence they must have had.

Pray for all state-supported Churches that they may wisely use their influence for good and avoid the temptations of worldly power. Pray too for Christians in this city today.

Lord Jesus Christ, who in this place caused your servant Constantine to become the ruler of a mighty empire, and later to favour those who believed in you: help us now and always to be so filled with your goodness and compassion, that all those in positions of authority may see in us the witness to your love.

Heavenly Father, who through the faith and courage of Eborius and his fellow Christians caused the light of the Gospel to shine in York: grant us so to walk in that light that by the pure witness of our faith and well-doing your kingdom may be enlarged.

Prayer for St Eborius' day,
1 August in the York Diocesan calendar

Re-establishing Christianity in York

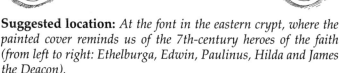

6th–7th centuries

Suggested location: *At the font in the eastern crypt, where the painted cover reminds us of the 7th-century heroes of the faith (from left to right: Ethelburga, Edwin, Paulinus, Hilda and James the Deacon).*

When the Romans left York, pagan invaders pushed the British Christians westwards into Wales, and we know nothing of any organized Christianity here in the 5th and 6th centuries. This led to missions at the beginning of the 7th century from two quarters.

The first was from the south when Bishop Paulinus was sent north by Augustine of Canterbury to accompany Ethelburga, daughter of the Kentish king, to marry Edwin, king of Northumbria. A condition of the marriage was that the queen would be allowed to practise her Christian faith. Eventually Paulinus persuaded Edwin to be baptized at York at Easter 627, in a little timber church built over a well – the first York Minster – soon after replaced by a large stone building. Also baptized with him were his household and family, among whom was probably Hilda his great-niece, who later founded a famous monastery in Whitby.

A heathen reaction followed the death of Edwin; Paulinus and Ethelburga fled south, but James the Deacon stayed with the fledgling Christian communities, and taught them the Roman method of chanting the psalms, the beginning of our long tradition of church music.

The second missionary wave came from Iona in Scotland. Celtic missionaries like St Aidan made their base at Lindisfarne, off the Northumbrian coast, and by their travelling and preaching helped to reignite the flame of the faith in the north-east.

Thank God for the courage of those who re-established the faith here and for your own baptism and those who brought you to it. This is a good occasion to renew your baptismal vows.

Do you turn to Christ?	**I turn to Christ**
Do you repent of your sins?	**I repent of my sins**
Do you renounce evil?	**I renounce evil**
Do you believe and trust in God the Father, who made the world?	**I believe and trust in him**
in his son Jesus Christ, who redeemed mankind?	**I believe and trust in him**
and in his Holy Spirit, who gives life to the people of God?	**I believe and trust in him**

Now must we hymn the Master of Heaven, the might of the Maker, the deeds of the Father, the thought of his heart. He, Lord everlasting, established of old the source of all wonders: creator all-holy, he hung the bright heaven, a roof high up-reared, o'er the children of men; the King of mankind then created for mortals the world in its beauty, the earth spread beneath them. He, Lord everlasting, omnipotent God.

Prayer of Caedmon,
cowherd poet to St Hilda of Whitby, *c* 680

The Great Saxon Age

8th–11th centuries

Suggested location: *In the Treasury you can look down on the portion of the outside wall of the Roman basilica where, after the Romans had gone, a gateway was made, suggesting that the Roman buildings were being reused by the Saxon inhabitants of York.*

The Saxon church was where the cathedra (the throne) of the Archbishop of York was placed, and so it became the cathedral, where many great church events have taken place.

Any church in Saxon times served by a team of clergy, who worshipped together and travelled to take services in surrounding villages, became called a Minster – a Saxon version of the Latin *monasterium*. The name has stuck with some churches, even where they have grown into great cathedrals or remained only small.

Saxon York also had a cathedral school, which became one of the most famous seats of learning in Christendom. Its teachers taught many future leaders of the Church, using the great Minster library. In 781 one of them, Alcuin, who had been Master of the Schools since 766, was called by Charlemagne to direct schooling throughout the Holy Roman Empire, and he is sometimes called the founder of modern education.

Although the Vikings came and caused much destruction around AD800, many settled down and embraced Christianity. One, Osketel, even became Archbishop (956–71). Many of the Christians of York of the 7th–11th centuries were buried in a huge cemetery under where the South Transept now is; some of their gravestones were discovered in 1967–72 and are on display here.

Thank God for the power of the Gospel to change lives, and for all missionaries.

Pray for all who work in Christian education, in universities, colleges and schools.

> *Eternal Light, shine into our hearts; Eternal Goodness, deliver us from evil; Eternal Power, be our support; Eternal Wisdom, scatter the darkness of our ignorance; Eternal Pity, have mercy upon us; that with all our heart and mind and strength we may seek your face and be brought by your infinite mercy into your holy presence; through Jesus Christ our Lord. Amen.*

Prayer of Alcuin

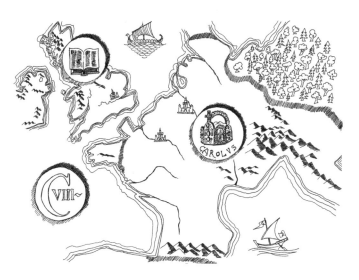

Norman vigour

11th–12th centuries

Suggested location: *Among the 11th-century foundations in the N or NW chambers of the Foundations; and among the 12th-century piers and St William's shrine in the western crypt.*

With the Norman victory over the Saxons in 1066 and with Thomas, a Norman archbishop sent from Bayeux in Normandy, the Saxon Minster and its clergy were swept away. The constitution of the Minster followed the Normandy pattern, with a Dean, a Precentor, a Treasurer and a Master of the Schools (later called Chancellor), and it has stayed much the same ever since. The new archbishop also built a huge new church. It was completed in about twenty years, no doubt using Saxon slave labour (much of its strong walls can be seen in the Foundations museum).

In 1154 the popular archbishop, William Fitzherbert, who had spent much of his archiepiscopate in exile while another held the office returned in triumph to York on the death of his enemies. On the way to the cathedral, crowds met him, and at the bridge over the River Ouse an accident occurred

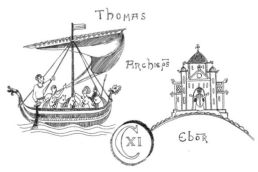

which was hailed as a miracle: in the crush, people fell off the bridge, yet no one was drowned. A few days later he suddenly and mysteriously died; this led to his eventual canonisation as St William of York, his body was transferred to a shrine behind the High Altar. Both the original tomb in the Nave and the new shrine were much visited by pilgrims throughout the rest of the Middle Ages.

In the 1170s it was decided to pull down the newly built East End and build a much bigger and wider Choir with a large crypt, parts of which survive in the western crypt underneath the present Choir. Rich panels of stained glass were placed in the windows, many of which were preserved when the Norman cathedral was eventually replaced; several of them can be seen today in the Nave clerestory: one at the bottom of the Five Sisters window and another, at eye level, in the Foundations museum.

Thank God for the Archbishops of York, and other Christian leaders through the centuries, and for the inspiration that their lives can still give us today.

Pray for all Christian ministers:

> *God our Father, shepherd and guide of all our faithful people: look with favour on those whom you have chosen to be pastors over your church, especially those whom we name before you…; grant that by word and example they may lead the people committed to their charge and with them come to your eternal kingdom.*

> *O God who dost gladden us with the merits and intercessions of the blessed William thy confessor and bishop, grant, we humbly beseech thee, that we who implore his virtues, may as a result receive the gift of thy grace; through Jesus Christ our Lord. Amen.*

Prayer for St William's Day
in the York medieval service books

The beginning of Gothic glory

13th century

In 1215 there arrived in York one of its most powerful archbishops ever, Walter Gray, formerly Chancellor to the king.
He set about tightening the organization of both diocese and
cathedral; he ensured that the stipends of the Chapter were
increased by adding new prebends (parishes whose
revenues provided the income for a canon). Because the
canons were so often absent from York they were each
provided with a deputy, a 'vicar'. These constituted the
College of Vicars Choral, with their own living quarters in
the Bedern. These junior clergy were the most obvious
presence at the Minster for centuries; their college was not
finally dissolved until 1936.

Parliament
in the
Chapter
House

Archbishop Gray also encouraged the Chapter to start pulling down the Norman cathedral and to replace it with an even bigger church in the contemporary, 'early English', style. This made use of clusters of narrow lancets, pointed windows, arcades of pointed arches, and the black-and-white effect of limestone and Purbeck 'marble'. The archbishop supplied much money for the first part of the project, the building of the present South Transept. He wished to be buried in the new transept, and at his death in 1255 was placed in a tomb in St Michael's Chapel, the earliest and one of the finest tombs in the Minster.

The work was carried on with the North Transept, financed largely through Chapter funds. The mistakes made in designing the gable of the South Transept were not repeated, and the gable end of the North Transept is a magnificent design, with the five great lancets containing the largest area of 13th-century *grissaille* glass in the world.

The Chapter House followed immediately (about 1270–80) in a slightly later style. It was built for the purpose for which it is still used today, for meetings of the Dean and Chapter, the governing body of the cathedral. Each of the seats is labelled with the name of the canon who currently sits there. It is one of the finest rooms in Europe; an inscription by the entrance proclaims in Latin: 'As the rose is the flower of flowers, so this is the house of houses'.

> *Incline thine ear to our prayers, O Lord, who humbly ask for thy mercy, that thou mayest place the souls of thy servants whom thou hast commanded to depart from this world in the region of peace and light and appoint them to be in the fellowship of thy saints; through Jesus Christ our Lord. Amen.*
>
> Prayer in the medieval York Missal
> for the souls of the faithful departed

Glory increased

14th century

At the beginning of the 14th century the work of building was continued with the Nave, wider and longer than the Norman one. It was built in the 'Decorated' style current in the 1290s, with developed tracery in the windows, soaring arches, and colourful picture panels in the windows, most of which are still in place.

The nobles of the English court contributed to the building of the Nave, and their heraldry is on stone shields over the arches and in the windows. Edward III married his queen in the Minster in 1328, and some years later their second son, William of Hatfield, was buried here, the only royal burial in the church. His monument is in the western end of the north Choir aisle.

A feature of the church that developed during this century was the multiplication of chantries, little altars against the pillars where junior priests were employed to say masses for the departed. These priests were given communal living quarters in 1461 with the foundation of St William's College, just to the east of the Minster. Today this is a venue for visitors coming out of the Minster, with a restaurant and toilets.

The Nave was built for processions and large services, and also for everyone to come in and feel at home in 'their Father's house'. Today it is where the main Sunday eucharist takes place, as do diocesan and provincial events. All visitors, whether pilgrims or tourists, are welcomed here with guides, leaflets and notices. Special provision is made for school parties, those with impaired sight or hearing, and those who come in wheelchairs.

This is part of a bidding prayer used here during the Middle Ages:

> *We shall make a special prayer unto God Almighty for the state of all holy church and for the peace of the realm. We shall pray for our father the Archbishop of this see; and for all the bishops, priests and clerks that have the cure of men's souls; for all other through whom God's service is maintained and upholden … and we shall pray for all other that have need of our prayers, that they turn them to the way that is most to God's pleasure, and that he give them good comfort; especially for them that are in sin, that God of his great mercy bring them soon to amendment; for them that suffer, that he release them of their pains; and for all faithful souls departed, that he bring them the bliss that ever shall last. And that these prayers may be heard and sped the sooner, every man and woman that there is, help them heartily, saying AMEN.*

The work completed

15th century

As the 14th century ended, a start was made on rebuilding the Choir, where the daily services had been maintained all through the construction of the new Nave. Starting at the East End, to postpone as long as possible the demolition of the Norman Choir, what you see now was built. A new magnificent shrine for St William was erected behind the High Altar, and crowds of pilgrims came up one aisle and down the other to pray at the shrine.

When the new Choir was almost complete, one of the piers of the old Central Tower collapsed, unable to cope with all the added weight. The tower was restored and heightened, and the western towers raised to their present heights. A great dedication service was held on 3 July 1472, the long work of 250 years largely complete.

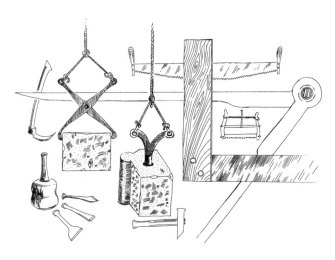

Grant that thine eyes may be open upon this house by day and by night ... be pleased to admit all men and women that come to adore thee in this place and graciously receive them ... hear and protect them that, ever happy and rejoicing in thy religion, they may persevere with constancy in the catholic and universal faith of the Holy Trinity ... As often as thy name shall be invoked in this thy house may our prayers be heard by thee, good Lord.

Part of a medieval prayer for the consecration of a church, as would have been used on 3 July 1472

Praise continued through change

16th–18th centuries

Then came the Reformation: the Church of England remained faithful to its Catholic heritage and at the same time reformed itself. It is Protestant in that it does not accept the supreme authority of the Pope, and as an Anglican Church it is part of a world-wide communion of similar churches. At the Reformation the cathedral worship continued and the Dean and Chapter remained in charge as before. Some things, however, were changed: the preaching would have mentioned the saving work of Christ more than the intercession of the Virgin Mary and the saints; the shrine of St William was dismantled and the chantry altars removed; the College of St William was abolished and the buildings handed over to secular use. A new feature gradually made its appearance, as canons married and the prebendal houses became family homes.

Instead of the many daily services, now there were only mattins and evensong, with the litany and communion on Sundays and holy days. The worship was now mainly in English, although cathedrals were among the churches allowed to continue using Latin, and that language has always featured in services. This was the great era of English church music, as magnificent settings of the communion service and the daily offices poured forth from such composers as Byrd, Gibbons, Tomkins and Purcell. No hymns were yet in use, but the psalms were chanted to a unique development of the Roman plainchant known as 'Anglican chant'. However, the feature of worship that most drew the crowds and was most talked about afterwards was the sermons, preached on a rota by the Dean and Canons, with extra ones at festivals and at times of national rejoicing or crisis.

In the 17th century York was royalist during the Civil War and was besieged for three months; during one service a cannon ball smashed in and ricocheted round the pillars. During the eleven years of Commonwealth the Minster clergy were sent away and a Puritan preacher installed, the organ and choir were silenced, and Anglican services forbidden.

All was restored in 1660. In 1686 the great brass lectern, now in the Nave, was given to the Minster, and the Bible has been read from it ever since.

> *Most bountiful and benign Lord God, we thy humble servants, freely redeemed and justified by the passion, death and resurrection of our Saviour, Jesu Christ, having our full trust of salvation therein, most humbly desire thee so to strengthen our faith and illumine us with thy grace, that we may walk and live in thy favour; and after this life to be partakers of thy glory in the everlasting kingdom of heaven, through our Lord Jesus Christ. So be it.*

Prayer ordered to be said at York Minster in 1574
and still used at every meeting of the Chapter

Crowds increase – a new role for the Minster

19th–20th centuries

In 1829, 1840 and 1984 large fires, in the Choir, the Nave and the South Transept respectively, destroyed the timber roofs and vaulting. The fire in 1829, deliberately started by a mentally unstable man, destroyed the magnificent medieval choir stalls and organ. After all three fires the public rallied round and restoration followed quickly, so that these parts of the Minster look now much as they did before the fires.

The latter part of the 19th century saw 'Military Sunday', a day for a crowded service attended by all the regiments stationed around York, and the musical festivals draw thousands of worshippers at a time. But in spite of being the seat of an archbishop, York Minster was always one of the poorer cathedrals, and it was a continuous struggle to find the money to keep this vast building in repair.

In 1967 cracks were spreading dangerously fast throughout the central tower area, and it was in danger of collapse. Huge excavation and engineering works were undertaken. The archaeological investigation revealed large parts of the Roman and Norman foundations and the Saxon cemetery, but no trace of the Saxon Minster. The engineering work surrounded the base of the piers with concrete, and the Minster was safe for future generations. A thanksgiving service was held in July 1972, exactly 500 years after the original consecration.

Then came the increase in tourism over the whole country and the crowds flocked in – over two million a year. The employees of the Dean and Chapter increased to 220 in number as staff were found both to restore the building and to help and inform visitors. Worshippers as well as tourists have increased, and communicant numbers in the last decades have risen dramatically. Cathedrals have become more and more important in the life of the Church as centres of mission and education; that is exactly what the word Minster has always implied.

> *Let me come into the church of God to meet the Spirit of God: not to give religion an hour but to live in the eternal: not to judge the words of a preacher but to draw life from the Word and Truth everlasting: not to be moved or soothed by music but to sing from the heart divine praises: not that my eyes roam over architecture or congregation but that my soul look up to the King in his beauty and my heart plead the needs of thy children.*

Prayer of Eric Milner-White, Dean of York 1941–63

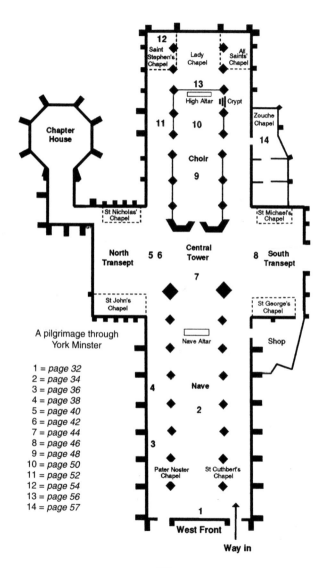

12
Saint Stephen's Chapel

Lady Chapel

All Saints' Chapel

Chapter House

13
High Altar | Crypt

Zouche Chapel

11

10

14

Choir

9

St Nicholas' Chapel

St Michael's Chapel

Central Tower

North Transept 5 6

8 **South Transept**

7

St John's Chapel

St George's Chapel

A pilgrimage through
York Minster

Shop

Nave Altar

Nave

4

2

3

Pater Noster Chapel

St Cuthbert's Chapel

1

West Front

Way in

A pilgrimage through York Minster

This pilgrimage starts at the back of the Nave in front of the great west doors [1]. Allow at least an hour, preferably an hour and a half. Do not hurry; it will be better to leave it unfinished, or divide it into two parts, rather than rush. Give plenty of time for your own thoughts and prayers.

At the West End [1]

In front of you is a tablet on the floor commemorating the founding of the cathedral in 627. You are sharing in a heritage of worship going back nearly 1400 years.

Take in the scene: the great arches, the vaulted roof with its carved bosses of the life of Jesus; the windows, many as old as the Nave in which you are standing, with their glorious colours. Beyond the Choir Screen you may be able to see the High Altar and, beyond that, the great east window.

When first built the Nave [2] was empty of most furniture, probably with many small chapels against the pillars or along the walls. Now it is a place of congregational worship for the main Sunday service and for many other special events like the Christmas carol service. Thousands of people come every year to worship, not all of whom are regular churchgoers; many more just walk around the Minster and enjoy its beauty.

Behind you are lists of the archbishops, deans, precentors, chancellors and treasurers who have maintained the worship of God here for many centuries, celebrating the sacraments and preaching his Word.

Think of the millions of people who, down the ages, have shared in the beauty of the great building, erected to the glory and praise of God.

Think of the builders, carpenters and glass painters, through whose skill the Minster was fashioned, and those whose gifts made it possible.

Pray for those who worship here every day or every Sunday, and for the thousands who come each year to special services.

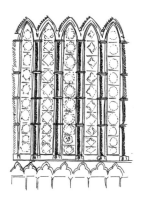

Look around you and pray for the people visiting the Minster today, the members of staff, and the clergy whom perhaps you and they will meet.

Let the splendour of the building lead you to adore the splendour of God himself:

> *Worthy of praise from every mouth,*
> *of confession from every tongue,*
> *of worship from every creature,*
> *is your glorious name, O Father,*
>   *Son, and Holy Spirit:*
> *You created the world, and by your grace and*
> *compassion you save the world.*

At the centre of the Nave [2]

*Walk forward to the central point of the Nave and turn round to face the great west window.

The glazing of the west window [1] was the climax of the building of the Nave. It was made in the year 1338, and paid for by Archbishop Melton. The glass is some of the finest of that period in the country.

There are three lines of pictures. At the bottom is a row of archbishops wearing their mitres. Many faces have been badly replaced, probably in the 18th century. The middle row shows the apostles. Look at the lovely figure of St John, third from the left. He is wearing a red robe and carries the palm of martyrdom in one hand and the eagle, his traditional symbol, in the other.

The third row up contains four pairs of pictures about Jesus. First on the left is the Annunciation. Then above the figure of St John is the Virgin Mary with the child Jesus and, facing her in the next panel, St Joseph, with an ox looking over his shoulder. Then come pictures of the Resurrection and the Ascension. Above the third row is a pair of pictures of the Coronation of the Virgin. She was – and is by many Christians today – believed to be so close to Jesus as mother and disciple that she was crowned as queen of heaven.

The stonework above was fashioned into the shape of a heart, and the window is sometimes called 'the Heart of Yorkshire'. More likely the builders wanted it to speak of the sacred heart of Jesus, symbol of his love.

Let the window remind you of the faith of the Church, of the first followers of Jesus who put their trust in him, and of the Church today, symbolized by the archbishops.

Thank God for the good news of the Gospel of Jesus:

for the obedience and humility of the Virgin Mary, through whom he was born,

for his coming to be 'God with us', Emmanuel, for us the human face of God,

for his life, and death on the cross,

and that he is now the Risen and Ascended Lord, to be with us for ever.

Think of the words in St John's Gospel:

God so loved the world that he gave his only begotten Son, that whoever believes in him should not perish but have eternal life.

Thank God too for his love in Christ:

May the love of the Lord Jesus draw us to himself
May the power of the Lord Jesus strengthen us in his service
May the joy of the Lord Jesus fill our lives today.

In the north Nave aisle: the penitentiary window [3]

*From where you are standing facing the west window, turn right and enter the north Nave aisle and find the third windown from the west.

Like most of the windows in this aisle, this was glazed about 1310 while the Nave was being rebuilt. At the bottom the Penitentiary is preaching what is a hell-fire sermon to the York people (look at his whip!). On the left a penitent makes his confession. This scene can be linked to the picture of the martyrdom of St Peter on the right at the top of the window. He was executed in Rome by the emperor Nero around the year 64; tradition has it that he was crucified upside down. Paulinus, the Bishop of York when the Minster was founded in 627, was an Italian, and presumably wanted to link the Minster with St Peter's in Rome from whence the mission team of which he was a member had been sent. The Minster has been St Peter's Cathedral ever since. Peter was one of the many Christians martyred during the early centuries of the Church. Rather than burn incense before a statue of the Roman emperor (although this meant little more to an average Roman than singing the National Anthem does to us today), they preferred to die for Christ as a witness to their belief that he, and not the emperor, was Lord.

This century has seen more Christian martyrs than any before, and people are still (for instance in Sudan) being martyred for their faith. The word 'martyr' means 'witness'. All Christians may not be called to die for Christ, but all are called to witness to him. This may be more difficult.

Thank God for all who have witnessed to Christ in life and death down the centuries.

Remember those martyred in this city at the time of the Reformation, some as Protestants, some as Recusants who wished to continue to worship in the old religion. Of the latter, Margaret Clitherow is the best known.

Pray
    for those who face death for their faith today,
    for those who find the pressures of ridicule and scorn too
        great for them to bear,
    for young people who go against the tide in following
        Christ,
    for those who just slide away from the faith.

God of grace,
your Church is built on Peter's faith;
grant that we, like him, forgiven and restored,
may overcome our weaknesses
and serve you without wavering,
now and ever.

New Zealand Prayer Book

In the north Nave aisle:
the Pilgrimage window [4]
*Move eastward along the north Nave aisle to the fifth window from the west (that is, miss one window).

The subject of the window is pilgrimage. At the bottom a knight and his lady, with their horses, are facing a splendid picture of St Peter, dressed as an archbishop, with church and key.

In the centre of the upper row is Christ crucified: pilgrimage calls for serious devotion. But pilgrims then and now also enjoy themselves, and there is much humour in this window. Look at the monkeys in the margins of the windows, on either side of the pilgrims; they are all looking upwards at flasks.

The strip of pictures at the foot of the left-hand window shows who they are. Read from right to left. First a monkey seated; then a darker monkey feeling his forehead, for he is ill; then a sick room table, and next a large monkey standing and looking at a flask, containing a sample given by the sick patient. The monkey is the doctor! But the patient dies; the coffin is preceded by monkeys carrying a cross and ringing a bell; at the left end of the strip, a fox (not clear) is reading the funeral service to a goose.

Enjoy the window and then think: it reflects the pilgrimage of life. For most of us (but not all) there is much happiness. The cross is a reminder that we cannot avoid suffering – and nor did Jesus.

The pilgrimage of death is also an event which we shall all have to face, but we do so knowing that the Risen Lord is Lord of life and death. Whatever is there, he is there.

Thank God for the way he has led you on your life's pilgrimage. Look back on the events of your life, both joyful and sorrowful. Think of that final offering of life in this world which you must one day make to God, and the more wonderful pilgrimage beyond this world.

Christ our Guide,
stay with us on our pilgrimage through life;
*   when we falter, encourage us;*
*   when we stumble, steady us;*
*   and when we have fallen, pick us up.*
Help us to become, step by step, more truly ourselves,
and remind us that you have travelled this way before us.

© Angela Ashwin, 1996

In the North transept:
the Five Sisters window [5]

*Continue eastwards along the north Nave aisle, and into the North Transept to look at the Five Sisters window.

The climax of the building of the transepts between 1220 and 1250 was the construction of this vast window. Each giant lancet is over 16 metres (50 feet) high, and 1.5 metres (over 4 feet) wide. The glass is original, in a style favoured by the influential Cistercian monks, who did not admit frivolous pictures or carvings into their churches. At first sight it seems to be no more than a jumble of tiny pieces, but as you look more closely you will see that the patterns in the glass are formed by the black outlines of the leadwork in the window. Perhaps this way of glazing in abstract patterns came to us from the Holy Land, where crusaders had seen windows like this in the mosques.

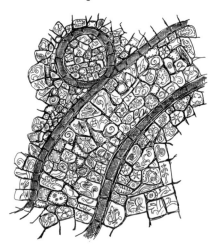

At the foot of the window is one picture, inserted at some unknown time, and older than the rest of the glass; it shows the prophet Habakkuk being brought by an angel to feed Daniel in prison (Dan. 14:33–42 or Bel and the Dragon, in the Apocrypha: verses 33–9).

Let the glory of this mosaic of glass, with its jewels of colour, speak to you of the mystery of God. He is 'Immortal, invisible, God only wise; in light inaccessible hid from our eyes'. Yet this is not the whole truth about God. Look at the panel at the foot of the window. He is a God who cares, and cares for each of us individually. And his love and care are no less a wonder than his mystery.

Look again at the way the jumble forms into patterns. Pray for all who can find no meaning in their lives. Jesus came to give us meaning and purpose.

He is the Way, to follow on the pilgrim way of life.
He is the Truth, who makes sense of the world, the people around us and ourselves.
He is the Life, not just existence but life worth living.

Pray for the mission of the Church,
for all who do not know Christ or do not love him.

Lord of eternity,
whose power is infinite,
whose days are without number,
and whose mercy is beyond our fathoming;
keep our faces turned always towards you,
so that each day we remember that life is your gift,
and the hour of death unknown.
And when we finally meet you face to face,
transform us in the fire of your love,
and receive us into your eternal kingdom.

© Angela Ashwin, 1996

The military chapels [6]

*Remain in the North Transept

In this part of the Minster you are surrounded by military chapels and war memorials. The Five Sisters window was last re-leaded in 1925 in honour of the women who fell in the First World War. Their names are recorded on the panels in the screen by the side of the Astronomical Clock. The clock is a memorial to the airmen and airwomen who died in the Second World War. On the left is the chapel of the King's Own Yorkshire Light Infantry.

*Now turn to face the South Transept

In the South Transept there is another regimental chapel and also the memorial to the choir members who fell in war.

The Rose window at the top of the South Transept wall, above the exit doors, also reminds us of war – the bloody civil conflict of the Wars of the Roses. Glazed about the year 1500, it can be said to commemorate the marriage of Henry of Lancaster (red rose) with Elizabeth of York (white rose), which signalled the end of the war since it contains red roses and the red and white Tudor rose adopted by Henry as his emblem as Henry VII.

The Rose window celebrates the making of peace.

Pray for all who are seeking peace in the world today; hold before God those countries torn by strife and violence.

'If you want peace, work for justice'

Pray for countries suffering from the injustice of the rich western society.

Each of the war memorials and military chapels commemorates men and women who gave their lives in war. Remember them with thanksgiving.

Pray for all who suffer through war today: the refugees; the wounded in body and mind; the bereaved.

> *Lord we pray for peace –*
> *not peace at any price but peace at your price.*
> *Make us and all your children so rich with your love,*
> *your generosity, your justice, that we can afford*
> *to pay the cost of your price.*

© Mothers' Union

> *Lead us from death to life; from falsehood to truth;*
> *lead us from despair to hope; from fear to trust;*
> *lead us from hate to love; from war to peace;*
> *let peace fill our hearts, our world, our universe.*

The Peace Prayer

The Choir Screen [7]

*Walk to the centre of the Minster, under the tower, and look at the stone screen at the entrance to the Choir.

On the stone screen stand the 15th-century statues of the kings of England from William the Conqueror to Henry VI. Most of them bear the symbols of power, and much of that power was oppressive. It was a violent age, and most of the kings were involved in conflicts, many of them with the French, the Welsh or the Scots.

The third king from the left, Stephen, stands out from the rest in having only a sword and no royal robe. He never completely ruled the country. King John, next to the central archway, was for many years excommunicated by the Pope; he looks appropriately angry. To the right of the Choir entrance, the kings seem to be more clearly differentiated; perhaps people still remembered what they looked like. The king at the far right of the screen, Henry VI, is different from the rest. Henry was popularly regarded as saintly and attracted devotion unwelcome to his successor Edward IV, who ordered the statue to be removed. Later the empty niche was filled by a statue of James I, which in its turn was removed and given to Ripon Cathedral where it now stands; a 19th-century statue of Henry VI was placed there in 1805.

Modern rulers may not carry the symbols of power, but in reality many hold far more power than the kings on the screen, both political and military power. Economic power also can change the lives of millions of people for better or worse. The power of the media manipulates minds in a way unknown in previous ages.

Pray for all people holding power; for rulers and statesmen, that they may have wisdom to know and courage to do what is right; pray particularly for the statesmen of the most powerful nations, that they may use their power responsibly. Pray too for the rulers of the poorer nations, many of these nations dragged so quickly into the modern world from conditions like those of the Middle Ages.

> *Grant us prudence in proportion to our power;*
> *wisdom in proportion to our science;*
> *and humaneness in proportion to our wealth and might;*
> *for your will, O God, is our peace.*

Conference of European Churches

The South Transept

*Move into the South Transept and look up at the roof.

The vaulted roof was constructed by the Minster crafts-men after the fire of 1984, which completely destroyed the previous roof and vault. The carved bosses reflect the theme of the ancient hymn, 'O all ye works of the Lord, bless ye the Lord'. Presided over by God the Father, on a great boss where the vault meets the tower arch, the works of creation praise the Lord: trees in and out of leaf; the sun and the moon; a well with a boy, a girl and a rabbit looking down it; a splendid fire-breathing dragon ('O ye fire and heat, bless ye the Lord!') and many more. The vault is best seen through the mirrors.

Near the wall on each side are bosses designed by children who won the *Blue Peter* television competition for the best designs. The easiest one to spot is the man in the moon, on the west side.

On the east side of the transept, in the aisle, is the mag-nificent canopied tomb of Archbishop Walter Gray, who ini-tiated the building of the transept in the year 1220. The Purbeck marble effigy is one of the finest 13th-century pieces in the country.

As you think of the vision which replaced a dark but solid Norman cathedral with a larger and lighter Gothic structure, reflect on Christ who is the light of the world.

The new vault reflects the wonder of the created world; of darkness and light; of water; of plants and animals.
Pray that we may not lay our clumsy fingers on God's cre-ation to destroy or defile it.

The *Blue Peter* bosses remind us of our children growing up in a confused and confusing world.
Pray for all who influence them; for parents and for teachers.

> Lord, your works are wonderful;
>   in wisdom you have made them all.
> Forgive us for madness that abuses the earth
>   for short-term ends,
> and give us wisdom to cherish and share,
>   with daring and delight
> the abundant gifts of our fragile planet.

© Angela Ashwin, 1996

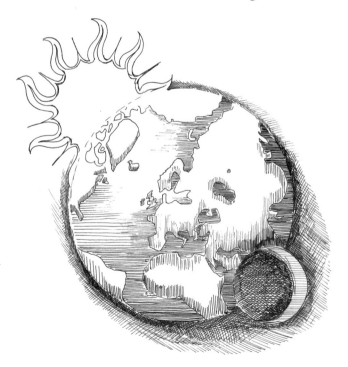

The Choir [9]

*Move back to the central tower and pass through the screen into the Choir. As you do, look upwards at the beautiful bosses in the archway of the screen.

You have moved into the part of the Minster which has formed the heart of its life down the centuries. Here in the Middle Ages the Dean and Canons met daily for the seven services of the Church. After the Reformation the tradition continued, with fewer services and in English instead of Latin. Now the service of Evensong is sung here on most days of the week by the boys or girls of the choir, eighteen of each, with twelve men singers, all highly trained and skilled in cathedral music, and directed by the Organist and his assistants.

Along the back row are the seats of the Dean and thirty Canons who at present make up the Chapter and are responsible for the work of the cathedral. Each canon's stall bears the name of the village where the prebendal estate was situated, from which until the last century the canon was paid. The Dean and Residentiary Canons, who work in the cathedral, sit at the west end of the Choir. The Archbishop's throne is at the east end on the south side; and there is a pulpit opposite on the north side.

Thank God for the heritage of cathedral worship and music down the ages, and for the Anglican tradition of singing, which is unique.

Pray for those who have day-to-day responsibility for the cathedral:
   for the Dean and Residentiary Canons,

for the Clerk to the Chapter and the administrative staff,

for those who serve on the floor of the Minster as police-
men, vergers, marshals and others,

for the staff of the bookshop and those who assist the
visitors,

for the many volunteers: guides, chaplains, embroiderers,
flower-arrangers, altar servers and bell-ringers,

for the staff of the stoneyard: masons, carvers, plumbers,
electricians, scaffolders, gardeners, etc.,

for the staff of the glass workshop,

for the organist and his assistants, and the children and
men of the choirs,

for the staff of the Minster school, and of the Centre for
School Visits,

for the staff and volunteers in the Minster Library.

> *How lovely is your dwelling place,*
> *O Lord of Hosts!*
> *My soul desires and longs*
> *to enter the courts of the Lord.*
> *My heart and my flesh sing joyfully*
> *to the living God.*
> *Happy are those who dwell in your house;*
> *they will sing your praises for ever.*

Psalm 84

The High Altar [10]

***Move along the Choir eastwards, and stand on the steps in front of the High Altar.**

At the centre of the worship of the cathedral is the Holy Communion service (the Eucharist) celebrated every day; in the Nave on Sunday morning, or in the Choir or in one of the chapels when there are smaller congregations.

When the present Choir was built in the late 14th century, the High Altar was situated where you are standing, lit on each side by the enormous windows in the eastern transepts telling the story of St Cuthbert (on the south side) and St William of York (on the north). Where the altar now stands, was the shrine of St William, to which many worshippers came to pray for healing. Look at the upper part of the St William window to see pictures of the shrine and of people praying there.

Close by the altar rails, on the north side, a brass plate commemorates the Malines Conversations between Roman Catholics and Anglicans, initiated in 1921 by Viscount Halifax and the Belgian Cardinal Archbishop of Malines (Mechelen). These conversations, although unofficial, paved the way for closer relationships between the two Churches.

Thank God for the Holy Communion, and for the wonder of Christ's coming to us in word and sacrament.

Pray that it may indeed become a sacrament of unity, binding together the whole of Christ's people.

Thank God for the vision of Lord Halifax and Cardinal Mercier, and for all who have sought, and are seeking, the unity of Christ's Church, as he wills and by the means he chooses.

Thank God for the many ways in which Christians are working together across the denominations, and pray for the group of lay Christians, of several denominations, who every Wednesday lead prayers for Healing and Peace in the Lady Chapel.

Gracious Father, we pray for your Church.
Fill it with your truth, and keep it in your peace.
        Where it is corrupt, purge it;
        where it is in error, direct it;
        where it is right, strengthen and confirm it;
        where it needs help, provide for it;
        where it is divided, heal it;
and unite it in your love,
through Jesus Christ our Saviour.

After William Laud, © Angela Ashwin, 1996

In the North Choir aisle: Archbishop Savage [11]

*Leave the Choir by the steps on the north side, and turn right in the north Choir aisle to the tomb of Archbishop Savage on the right.

Thomas Savage was one of the last archbishops before the Reformation. He is lying comfortably, unaware of the storms about to break over the Church. Above his tomb, his chantry chapel, probably destroyed in the fire of 1829, has been rebuilt. It was one of over 60 chantries in the medieval Minster, where masses were said for the souls of the departed.

There are many other memorials to archbishops in this part of the Minster, and also to notable lay people like Sir Henry Belassis and his wife, on the wall opposite Archbishop Savage. They lived at the end of the reign of Queen Elizabeth I. Above the two main figures, and between them, is a charming carving of a cherub blowing bubbles, reminding us of the uncertainty of our human lives.

Thank God for all who have served the Minster and the Church in Northern England down the ages.
Pray for the present Archbishops of York and Canterbury, and for the other bishops of the Church of England and for its clergy and laypeople, and for the bishops, clergy and lay people of all the churches throughout the world with which it is in full communion.

Pray too for the leaders of other churches:
> for the Pope,
> for the bishops and clergy of the Roman Catholic Church in England,
> for the Orthodox Churches and the other ancient churches of the east,

for the Methodist Church and the churches of the Lutheran and Reformed traditions.

Pray for any church leaders whom you know personally.

Remember all who, having served Christ here, have departed this life, commending them to his keeping, in the faith of the Resurrection. Think of those you have known and loved, and of those for whom you are grateful.

> *Father of all, we pray to you for those we love but see no longer.*
> *Grant them your peace.*
> *Let light perpetual shine upon them;*
> *and in your loving wisdom and almighty power,*
> *work in them the good purpose of your perfect will.*
> *Through Jesus Christ our Lord.*

1928 Prayer Book

St Stephen's Chapel [12]

*Walk forward to the east end of the north Choir aisle and enter St Stephen's Chapel.

You may like to relax for a moment and look at the beautiful kneelers, each unique, depicting the flowers of the various continents. They were made by the Minster Broderers.

Behind the altar is a vivid representation of the crucifixion, made for the High Altar in 1875, and moved to this position in 1937. Above, in the east window, is another depiction of the crucifixion in glass.

In the second window from the east, on the north side of the chapel, are three fine 14th-century figures of St Stephen, the first Christian martyr (holding stones), St Christopher and St Lawrence (holding a grid-iron). On the right at the front of the chapel is a bust of Mother Teresa of Calcutta.

Let the pictures of the two martyrs remind you of the suffering world; let the reredos and the window above speak to you of Jesus' life and death; let the figure of St Christopher and the bust of Mother Teresa recall all who minister to those who suffer.

You may like to sit quietly and name before God any people you know about who are suffering.

Pray too for those who work to relieve suffering; remember your own doctor.

Pray for the work of hospitals and hospices and those who minister to the sick.

Remember people who are in pain; those with distressing diseases; those awaiting operations; those who are

approaching death.

Lord Jesus, by the loneliness of your suffering on the cross,
be near to all who are desolate,
and in pain or sorrow;
Let your presence transform their sorrow into comfort,
and their loneliness into fellowship with you;
for the sake of your tender mercy.   George Appleton

Make us worthy, Lord, to serve our fellow human beings
who live and die in poverty and hunger.
Give them through our hands this day their daily bread,
and by our understanding love give peace and joy.
                                        Mother Teresa, adapted

The Lady Chapel [13]

*Move into the Lady Chapel and sit down in the row of seats at the back.

When the Choir was built in the 14th century there was an altar to the Virgin Mary in this chapel, to which pilgrims would come as they passed up the steps which were then in the screen to reach the shrine of St William behind the High Altar.

The chapel is dominated by the great east window, as large as a tennis court, glazed between 1405 and 1408. The theme is set by the topmost panel where God holds a book inscribed 'I am Alpha and Omega' – the first and last letters of the Greek alphabet (Rev. 1:8). The theme is worked out in the square panels which make up most of the window. Above the gallery that runs across the window are three lines of pictures telling the Bible story of the beginning of our existence (from the floor you can only see the top line clearly, but there are paintings of the three lines on the panel displayed on the right of the chapel). In the first line look for God making the world (left), including the birds and fish (centre) and Adam and Eve (right) who have sinned and are cast out of the garden.

Beneath the gallery are pictures of the end of time, a pictorial representation of the Book of Revelation which concludes the Bible. At the bottom are bishops and kings of the northern church, with Bishop Skirlaugh of Durham, the donor of the window (centre).

Ponder the message of the window that God is the God of the whole of human history, and therefore Bishop Skirlaugh's God and your God too! The End is not yet but the dreams and visions of the Book of Revelation declare that the climax of history will not be the final folly of the human race but the final triumph of God's purpose. The sign of that victory is the triumph of love in the cross of Christ, proclaimed by the Resurrection. Christ Jesus is the living Lord. He calls each and every person, he calls you – to take your place on the stage of human history and, where you are, to seek God's will.

Thank God for giving you yourself and all you have and are;
for the faith and hope he has given you in Jesus Christ;
for calling you to his service.

> *For all that has been – thanks!*
> *To all that shall be – Yes!*

Dag Hammerskjöld

> *Teach us, good Lord, to serve you as you deserve;*
> *to give and not to count the cost;*
> *to fight and not to heed the wounds;*
> *to toil and not to seek for rest;*
> *to labour and not to ask for any reward,*
> *save that of knowing that we do your will.*

St Ignatius Loyola

*At the end of the pilgrimage you may wish to light a candle, or to go into the Zouche chapel [14] (through a door on the left of the south choir aisle) where you can sit and pray quietly.

*If you would like to visit the Foundations and crypts in a prayerful way, see the suggestions on page 12–18.

A pilgrim path through the City of York

Leave York Minster by the South Transept door. Turn right from the transept and note the tablet by the entrance to the Minster shop to **Miles Coverdale**, translator of the Bible into English. Opposite is the church of **St Michael-le-Belfry**, which may lie over the foundations of the Anglo-Saxon cathedral; it was the scene of the notable ministry of David Watson, an Anglican preacher and priest.

Continue into Duncombe Place. On the right is **St Wilfrid's Roman Catholic Church** (open). Go over the cross-roads to Museum Street. On the right is the remnant of **St Leonard's Hospital**, closed at the Reformation. Turn right into Museum Gardens, pass the ruins of the Benedictine **Abbey of St Mary**, and leave the gardens into Marygate. On the right is **St Olave's Church** (open); the earlier church, also dedicated to the Norwegian warrior saint, is mentioned in the Anglo-Saxon Chronicle.

Walk down Marygate to the river and turn left along the riverside to reach Lendal Bridge. Climb the cobbled road and then cross right into Lendal to reach St Helen's Square (**Church** to the left, open).

Continue along Coney Street, passing **St Martin's Church** (open sometimes) which has a fine 14th-century window of the saint. Coney Street passes into Spurriergate and here is **St Michael's Church**, now the Spurriergate Centre (fine interior; refreshments). Turn right to Ouse Bridge.

Do not cross the bridge, but go left down steps to the riverside. To the left was the Franciscan Friary. Continuing to St George's Field, turn left along the city wall to reach **Clifford's Tower**, all that is left of York Castle. Here the York

Jews perished in 1190 (open; English Heritage). Leave the tower by turning left across the car park to Castlegate. On the right is **St Mary's Church**, with its 11th-century foundation stone. At the top of the street, left, is Friargate, home of the York Quaker Meeting for 200 years and more.

Turn right into Coppergate, passing **All Saints Pavement** on the left (open; entrance in High Ousegate). Cross Parliament Street to the Pavement, and turn left into the Shambles. The shrine chapel of **St Margaret Clitherow** (open) is on the left. At the end of the Shambles, turn left into Newgate. On the right is a **stone building** where John Wesley preached, and where the Methodists worshipped from 1753 to 1759.

Return to King's Square and at the crossroads turn right into Goodramgate. On the left a gateway leads to **Holy Trinity Church** (open), which has medieval glass and 18th-century furnishings, reminders of Christian worship in York down the centuries. Continue along Goodramgate and turn left to return to the Minster.

Children in a Minster

A kaleidoscopic crocodile of schoolgirls,
in reds, golds, blues, beige, purple, green, dun frocks
soiled, unsoiled, pressed, creased,
short, long; stockinged, socked,
barelegged;
with dark hair, flaxen, auburn, mousy, long, pigtailed,
short,
hatless, felt-hatted, straw-hatted,
with chinstraps, without.
And boys
with slung satchels, grub-filled knapsacks
and notebooks ready, winding through the Minster;
a few, gazing at the glass,
some, flabbergasted at its hugeness,
most, with the child's witless bravery,
unawed by the spacious,
graceful beauty;
surprised nudges, repressed giggles,
sometimes a gasp of wonder;
winding; slowly;
occasionally listening to an
expounding mistress or master:
winding slowly;
brushing the smaller, little groups of adults

a kaleidoscopic crocodile

and, at its end,
a diminutive, hatless straggler.

If
in life's haste,
you would save
your turgid, rushing soul,
be like her,
unhurried, aware, wondering;
fresh, innocent,
with pencil ready,
looking

… looking.

For further information

To book a **group pilgrimage**, contact the Visitors Officer at the Chapter Office, tel. (01904) 639347. There are no fees for pilgrimage parties. Service papers and hymn sheets are provided. Early booking is desirable, as the Minster is well used for other events during summer evenings.

For individual pilgrimages a 'Walk-round pilgrimage Guide' leaflet is obtainable free of charge from the Minster Information desks.

Publications about the Minster

A free leaflet, giving brief details about the Minster, is available at the desk at the west end and elsewhere; at the desk it is available in a number of languages.

Inexpensive guide books and booklets are available from the Minster shop, situated near the south transept. A selection would include:

– *The Guide Book to York Minster*; quite detailed.
– *York Minster*, the Pitkin guide.
– *York Minster*, the Scala Press; pictures and text.

Publications about pilgrimage:

Pilgrims, by Stephen Platten, HarperCollins 1996; introduces pilgrimage, past and present.

The Book of a Thousand Prayers, compiled by Angela Ashwin, Marshall Pickering 1996.

Prayers for Pilgrims, Wild Goose Publications, the Iona Community.

Pilgrimage Yesterday and Today: why? where? how? by J. G. Davies, SCM Press 1988; gives much historical detail and examines the theology of pilgrimage.